IMAGES
of America

PEABODY

Major General Grenville Dodge, Post 50, Grand Army of the Republic, proposed a memorial to the soldiers and sailors of the Civil War in 1879. The sum of $8,000 was procured by the town for its construction. The 50-foot high monument was constructed by the Hallowell Granite Company, and the dedication took place on November 10, 1881.

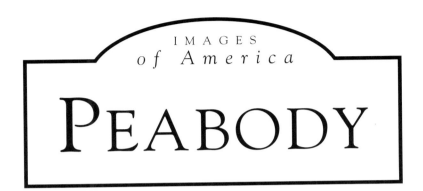

IMAGES
of America

PEABODY

Stephen J. Schier and Kenneth C. Turino

ARCADIA

First published 1997. Reprinted 1998
Copyright © Stephen J. Schier and Kenneth C. Turino, 1997

ISBN 0-7524-0548-9

Published by Arcadia Publishing,
an imprint of Tempus Publishing, Inc.
2 Cumberland Street, Charleston SC 29401.
Printed in Great Britain

Library of Congress Cataloging-in-Publication Data applied for

The seal of the city of Peabody was created in 1917. Prior to this no official seal existed. The design was ordained by the city council as follows: "The Seal of the City of Peabody shall be a circular die containing the following—a facsimile of the exterior of the Peabody Institute in Peabody together with the following inscription—South Danvers, 1855, Town of Peabody 1868: City of Peabody 1916 and that the City Clerk be the custodian thereof."

Contents

This photograph of the Soldiers Monument and the South Congregational Church in Peabody Square had to have been taken in 1897–98, the one year photographer F.C. Goodridge was in business on Main Street in Peabody. The city directories list no other photographers for the entire 1890s. This points to the town's dependency on Salem.

Acknowledgments

The authors wish to thank all those individuals and institutions that assisted with research, as well as locating and lending photographs. The Peabody Historical Society deserves special mention. Under the leadership of Rosa Drysdale, the Society has amassed an outstanding collection of photographs and a group of dedicated volunteers. This publication could not have been completed without the help of assistant librarian/archivist Barbara Doucette, who was invaluable in assisting the authors with their research. Joseph M. Donlon, vice-president, also assisted, particularly with the fire and police department images. The Peabody Historical Society is especially fortunate to own a large collection of photographs taken by well-known photographer H. Ray Wallman, who has documented the city for decades. Unless otherwise noted, photographs in this book are from the collection of the Peabody Historical Society.

Many others were of great help. Thanks must go to Lil Limon of the North Shore Jewish Historical Society in Lynn, who generously lent photographs. Anna Ortins took time out from working on her Portuguese cookbook to supply information and photographs on Peabody's large Portuguese community. Henry R. Theriault, a private collector, and owner of The Sea Witch souvenir shop in Salem, MA, allowed the use of images from his collection. Elaine F. Cutler, Sandra DeGrazia, Sally Nicosia, and Mr. and Mrs. Roger Slate lent family photographs, as did John Hardy Wright. Diner photographs were lent by Gary Thomas. Lastly, the authors wish to thank Fay Greenleaf, who typed the manuscript and provided editorial assistance, and Chris, Ben, and Sally Mathias and Borinous Schier for their encouragement, patience, and support.

Introduction

The city of Peabody, MA, has undergone a number of vicissitudes in its naming over its long and illustrious history. From 1630 to 1710 this vast area was part of Salem. The agrarian settlement was known as Brooksby. With the impending establishment of a new meetinghouse, a petition was presented to the General Court by the townspeople for a new and separate precinct. After much debate, both houses of the legislature approved this new formation in November of 1710. From 1710 to 1752 the Brooksby area was known as the middle precinct. In 1752 the village parish of Danvers and the middle precinct agreed to form a new district. The middle precinct became first known as Second Parish in the District of Danvers, then as the South Parish in Danvers, and finally South Danvers. Because of different geographical, manufacturing, and business concerns between North and South Danvers, a petition for separation of the two districts was granted by the state legislature in 1855.

The town of South Danvers was incorporated on May 18, 1866. During its infancy as a town, people not familiar with the area were confused with the names Danvers and South Danvers. Seeking its own identity as a town, the name was changed by referendum to Peabody in 1868, in honor of George Peabody (1795–1869), the philanthropic native son.

The confines of Peabody are dotted with scenic bodies of water in the form of lakes, ponds, rivers, and reservoirs. Some of the more well-known areas are Suntaug Lake, Brown's Pond, Spring Pond, Crystal Lake, the Devils Dishful Pond, Cedar Pond, and Bartholomew Pond. The Ipswich, Waters, and North Rivers proved to be an asset to the city's development as a great manufacturing center.

In the early days of Peabody's industrial development, there were glassworks, potteries, cotton and woolen mills, quarries, a bleachery, a glue works, and various other businesses that supported its main product, leather. The abundance of clean fresh water proved ideal for the tanning of leather. During its heyday in the late 1800s and early 1900s, Peabody became the largest producer of leather in the world. Peabody is aptly called the Leather City.

After the turn of the twentieth century, the demand for unskilled laborers in the tanneries resulted in a great influx of immigrants. The first groups to arrive were the Turks and Greeks, who were followed by the Polish, Portuguese, and Russians who, along with the Irish and French Canadians who had arrived earlier, gave the city a cosmopolitan appearance.

The leather industry has dwindled to only a few enterprises. The manufacturing base of the city has shifted to other areas, some within the confines of the Centennial and Industrial Park.

Peabody today is a melting pot of various nationalities, has a vibrant downtown area, and can lay claim to having one of the largest shopping malls in New England. At the same time, the city retains some of its seventeenth-century charm in Brooksby Farm, where the first period Felton houses still stand and the orchards continue to produce an abundance of fruit.

The photographs for this book, over two hundred images, many of which have never before been published, chronicle the growth of Peabody.

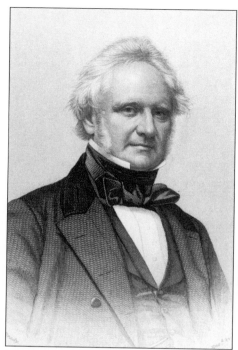

A steel engraving of George Peabody (1795–1869) by the New York artist John Chester Buttre (1821–1893), after a photograph by the pioneer photographer Mathew B. Brady (c. 1823–1896.)

The Lexington Monument is pictured here, when it was located at the corner of Washington and Main Streets. The obelisk-shaped memorial, with a plinth base, was made of granite quarried in Peabody. Completed in 1837, the original inscriptions were carved on tablets of Italian marble and later replaced by bronze. Embossed on the East tablet is "Battle of Lexington April 19th, 1775. Samuel Cook age 33; Benj. Daland 25; George Southwick 25; Jothan Webb 22; Henry Jacobs 22; Ebenr. Goldthwait 22; Perley Putnam 21—Citizens of Danvers fell on that day. PRO PATRIA MORI. Embossed on the West tablet. Erected by Citizens of Danvers on the 60th Anniversary 1835." In 1985, the monument was moved to its present location at the corner of Washington and Sewell Streets.

One
George Peabody

On February 18, 1795, George Peabody was born to Thomas and Judith Dodge Peabody. In 1811, he moved from Peabody to Newburyport, MA. A year later, he moved to Georgetown in the District of Columbia. In 1814, he became a partner with Elisha Riggs, a dry-goods merchant, and the firm Riggs and Peabody moved to Baltimore. In 1837, he established himself at Wanford Court, England, as a merchant and money broker, and was soon head of one of the largest mercantile concerns in the world. In 1854, Peabody retired and dedicated himself to philanthropy. By the time of his death in London on November 4, 1869, he had donated more than $8 million to philanthropic causes.

This is a photograph of the George Peabody Birthplace, at 205 Washington Street. It is a simple wood-frame Colonial structure with a pitched roof, clapboard siding, hinged painted shutters, and projecting front pavilion. The photograph was probably taken after George Peabody's funeral on February 8, 1870. The day of the funeral, a severe snowstorm developed and made traveling difficult for the procession and spectators alike.

An interior view of the front parlor of the George Peabody House is shown here as it appeared c. 1880. This room on the first floor to the right of the front door is said to have been the room where George Peabody was born. Except for a brief hiatus due to financial difficulties, the home was in the Peabody family from 1784 to 1832. The photograph shows a typical eclectic Victorian interior cluttered with ornate furniture, photographs, and various gewgaws.

Pictured here is the red brick and brownstone Peabody Institute Library, at 82 Main Street. It was built in 1852 through the generosity of George Peabody, whose combined monetary gifts totaled $200,000. The cornerstone was laid on August 20, 1852, and the dedication took place two years later, on September 29, 1854. In 1867–68, the Institute was enlarged and a tower was added through the generosity of benefactress Mrs. Eliza Sutton. She established a reference library as a memorial to her son, Eben Dale Sutton, who died in 1862. The building is decorated in funeral bunting for George Peabody's funeral, February 1–8, 1870. (Photograph courtesy of Henry R. Theriault.)

An interior view of the Peabody Institute Library, c. 1899, shows a dazzling display of gifts, awards, letters, and mementos all given to the citizens of Peabody by the philanthropist George Peabody. Included is a priceless gold and jeweled porcelain miniature of Queen Victoria, two gold boxes from the city of London and the Fishmonger Company, a Congressional gold medal, a letter from Queen Victoria, and various other awards and proclamations.

On October 9, 1856, George Peabody was honored by his home town of Danvers. Peabody regarded the whole of the old town as one, and accepted joint invitations from the two towns. The huge procession in South Danvers was over a mile long, and included more than 1,700 school children. This lithograph depicts the parade marching through Peabody Square. The parade concluded at the Peabody Institute, and the gala ended with a dinner reception for 1,200 guests under a gigantic tent.

The parade passes by the Warren Bank Building on Main Street. This house of banking, incorporated in 1832, was the second to be established in Peabody. It was named after General Joseph Warren, who was killed at the battle of Bunker Hill in Charlestown, MA.

An escort of fireman with a hand pumper and hose reel are shown as they pass the Lexington Battle monument on Main Street, during the parade honoring George Peabody. The dwelling in the center is the residence of the Hon. Robert S. Daniels.

The parade passes the Main Street residence of Mr. and Mrs. Thomas A. Sweetser. The house was decorated under a canopy of American flags, along with a fine portrait of Sylvester Proctor, which was painted by Mrs. Sweetser. Under the upper windows was a beautiful arrangement of dahlias of various colors forming the name "George Peabody."

A woodblock engraving from Harpers Weekly depicts the catafalque and casket of George Peabody. The remains of Peabody laid in state at the Peabody Institute from February 1–8, 1870. Thousands of people came to pay their respects. Among the notables in attendance was Prince Albert, son of Queen Victoria. The funeral was held at the South Congregational Church on February 8, 1870.

The George Peabody Tomb is at Harmony Grove Cemetery on the Peabody-Salem line. Mr. Peabody's last request was to be buried in his beloved native town, near the graves of his parents. His remains were first deposited in Westminster Abbey from November 12 to December 11, 1869. The remains were shipped to America on board Queen Victoria's largest ship, the HMS *Monarch*. At Harmony Grove Cemetery, the casket was temporarily placed in Joseph Peabody's tomb until this impressive granite sarcophagus memorial could be erected by the executors of his estate. (Photograph courtesy of Henry R. Theriault.)

Two
Houses

The King house, at the corner of Lowell and Forest Streets, was originally built in 1846 by Samuel King. The house was said to have been a stop on the Underground Railroad prior to the Civil War. Located next to the dwelling is the King Cemetery.

The Derby Summer House was built by Samuel McIntire (1757–1811) the noted architect of Salem, for Elias Haskett Derby (1739–1799) in 1793. It remained in Peabody at Osborn Farm until the spring of 1901, when Mrs. William C. Endicott purchased it and removed it to her summer estate, Glen Magna, in Danvers, Massachusetts, a distance of four miles. There is a figure at the front and rear of the two-story building, and four neoclassical urns at each corner. The frontal figure depicts a man whetting his scythe, and the corresponding figure is of a milkmaid with a milk pail in her hand.

The Derby-Crowinshield-Endicott-Osborn mansion on Andover Street was the summer residence of Elias Haskett Derby. The estate had elaborate gardens and very extensive greenhouses. In 1805, the heirs of Elias Haskett Derby sold the farm to Jacob Crowinshield (1770–1808). His daughter, Mary Crowinshield Endicott owned the property until 1832, when she sold it to Amos King. The property remained in his possession until 1848. In March of that year the farm, which then contained 39 acres, was sold to Kendall Osborn Sr. and remained in the Osborn family until 1925. The dwelling was razed in the 1970s.

A part of the rambling Osborn Farm barn was moved from Derby Wharf in Salem, MA, during the late eighteenth century. The barn, designed by Samuel McIntire, was located on the westerly side of the mansion house. By 1925 the barn had fallen into disrepair and was razed by Batchelder and Morrissy, the developers of Osborn Heights. In 1925 only 10 acres remained of this once sprawling estate of several hundred acres. The main access to the property was known as Apple Tree Lane. The name was later changed to Buttonwood Lane, where many fine dwellings were erected.

The Flint-King House, located at 629 Lowell Street. In 1824, Daniel P. King (1801–1850) married Sarah P. Flint, and they took up residence at this farmhouse, which was Sarah's inheritance. The Hon. Daniel P. King was a state senator, and in 1843 was elected to Congress as a representative from the Essex District, a post in which he served with distinction until his death. Today this building is known as the Lakeside School.

The Daniel Epes House was built c. 1702. Additions were made later, and in 1891 the house was moved from the Rogers farm to Washington Street.

This is the Quint Property, at State and Sutton Streets. Nicholas Morrill Quint came to Peabody after his graduation from Fryeburg Academy in Maine in 1857. He was employed as a foreman of the large farm of Hazen Ayer on Sutton Street. Quint later became owner of the farm. He married Sally Putnam in 1866, and was responsible for dividing the Ayer Farm into streets and house lots. He was also Peabody's representative to the state legislature for several terms, trustee of the Warren National Bank, and a director of the Peabody Co-Operative Bank. Quint died October 30, 1906, at which time this property was sold. (Photograph courtesy of his granddaughter, Ruth F. (Lord) Spicer.)

This photograph, taken in 1907, shows the home of farmer George H. Hutchinson on Russell Street, in West Peabody. Shown here are the hay wagons packed for moving.

The headquarters of the Peabody Historical Society are located at 35 Washington Street. The house was the home of General Gideon Foster (1749–1845), captain of a company of Minutemen from South Danvers who fought at the Battle of Lexington, on April 19, 1775. He was very prominent in local affairs, at one time owning a grist mill, a bark mill for the tanning of leather, and a chocolate mill, all located in the Foster Street area. The home has been the headquarters of the Peabody Historical Society since 1916. The dwelling now houses the Society's many collections, with each room featuring displays relating to Peabody's historic past.

The Parson Benjamin Prescott (1687–1777) House, at 72 Central Street, was built c. 1749. The house was a wedding present for the sister of Sir William Pepperill. Mary Pepperill (born 1696) was the third wife of Parson Prescott, whom she married in 1748. Over the years this large dwelling of fifteen rooms has had a variety of owners. The house was divided, with the southern and northern halves being under separate ownership. The house was destroyed by fire and razed. Pictured are, from left to right: Mrs. Henry Buxton, unknown, Mary Jane Buxton, owner, Joshua Buxton (seated), and Henry Buxton. The Prescott Apartments occupy this site today.

This quaint gambrel roof cottage known as the Old Bowditch House, on Central Street at Wilson Square, was the boyhood home of the eminent mathematician and author Nathaniel Bowditch (1773–1838). Bowditch was born in Salem, but due to financial difficulties the family moved to South Danvers in 1775. The family lived in this cottage for several years. Across the street from the Bowditch home was a school where young Nathaniel received rudimentary instructions in reading, writing and arithmetic. In 1802 Bowditch wrote the *New American Practical Navigator*, which is still in use today. (Photograph courtesy of Borinous Schier.)

In 1919 the house and land of the Asa Bushby House, then located at 75 Central Street, were purchased by the city of Peabody for the expansion of the high school. The house was moved to 17 North Central Street, its present location. Asa Bushby was born in South Danvers on June 9, 1834. He was a largely self taught portrait painter. Bushby was painting portraits in the Peabody area as early as 1856. After returning from the Civil War, he turned to photography, opening a studio in Peabody, then moving to Lynn, and later to Boston. He finally settled in Tacoma, WA, toward the end of the 1880s, and died there on June 31, 1897.

This fashionable Italianate two and a half story dwelling, the home of Harvey and Angeline (Larrabee) Buxton, at 21 Andover Street, had an outhouse in the rear surrounded by fruit trees.

Prospect Street, at the corner of Andover Street, was the home of Nathan Felton (1770–1829). Nathan Felton was town clerk from 1801 to 1828. He served both Danvers and what is present-day Peabody. This two-and-one-half-story home had a projecting front pavilion for a front entryway. The one story addition with its brick foundation was probably the kitchen.

The Thomas H. Sawyer House, at 83 Lowell Street at the corner of Sawyer Street, is shown here in the mid-1880s. Mr. Sawyer, a dealer in provisions, owned this well-proportioned Federal-style home with an attached barn. The tall square brick chimney in the background is that of the Sanger Glue Factory, later the site of the A.C. Lawrence Leather Company.

The Peabody Almshouse was located on Lynnfield Street. In 1809 the town of Danvers purchased the Nathaniel Nurse farm, which encompassed more than 200 acres. In 1844 this sturdy red brick and granite structure was built on the former Nurse property. This building was used by the city until 1963. Later, it was incorporated into the Peabody Industrial Park for use in the business sector.

This Colonial-style dwelling at 109 Central Street with a huge central chimney and impressive front entry was the home of Henry Varney Buxton and his wife Mary Eastman. The building was demolished in 1926 to make way for the Farnsworth School. .

The Edward P. Barrett House at 110 Central Street, shown in this *c.* 1900 photograph. The central entryway of this home featured double front doors with a fashionable Italianate bracketed canopy overhead. The windows all had working shutters capped by bracketed flat pediments. The simple free-standing barn had wide sliding doors and a narrow transom light window. Mr. Barrett owned the Mowry and Phillips Brass Foundry at 108 North Street in Boston.

The Nathaniel Felton Jr. House on Felton Street was built *c.* 1683. This dwelling, the neighboring Smith Apple Barn, the Orchard House, and an eight and one-half acre parcel of land were bequeathed to the Peabody Historical Society in 1976 by Mrs. Austin Smith, the widow of the former owner. This building, shown here *c.* 1914, is on the National Register of Historic Places. The Nathaniel Felton Jr. House is available to other organizations, civic groups, and the general public for functions at a nominal fee.

The *c.* 1920 photograph shows the Nathaniel Felton Sr. House, built in 1644 on Felton's Hill, the oldest house in Peabody still standing. This served as the ancestral home of the Feltons for generations. From the beginning of the twentieth century, the Smith family owned the Felton homestead and operated the adjoining apple orchards as part of their family business, Brooksby Farm. This house was given to the Peabody Historical Society in 1980 by Miss Janet Smith.

This *c.* 1910 photograph shows the Ernest A. Woelfel House, 22 Osborn Street. The building at the rear of the barn was the leather finishing factory of E.A. Woelfel. The factory, located on Pierpont Street, produced fancy and embossed leather from various reptilian and animal hides.

The Clark Wilson House, 5 Andover Street at Wilson Street, was built *c.* 1795. In the latter half of the nineteenth century this home was enlarged and remodeled in the Second Empire Victorian style by its owner, Daniel Bolles Lord. Today the first floor is used for retail business and the upper stories serve as apartments. This photograph was taken in 1899, when the Lord family occupied the house.

The Clerk House at 12 Elm Street, shown here in *c.* 1890 photograph, was home of the prosperous leather manufacturer George Clerk. For over fifty years Clerk, a native of Great Britain, was involved with the Peabody leather industry.

This *c.* 1920 photograph shows the Frank L. Pitman family on the front stairs of 20 Home Street. This was the first house built off Sutton Street by Mr. Pitman, a Nova Scotian housewright and carpenter. From left to right are Helen Symonds, Grace Maude Cone, Irving Goodell, Evelyn Newhall, Frank Leslie, Doris Elliott, Eunice Maude, and Bertha Bartlett Pitman. A poem the children made up refers to a teacher they were evidently not fond of "An eagle flew from North to South, with Brother Bowen in his mouth- and when he saw he had a fool, he dropped him at the Wallis School." (Photograph courtesy of John Hardy Wright.)

Mayor O'Donnell bids farewell to St. Joseph's Juniorate Brothers at a reception at the historic Oak Hill mansion. The mansion was built *c.* 1800 for Captain Nathaniel West and his wife, Elizabeth Derby West. The dwelling had magnificent architectural features and furnishings designed and carved by Samuel McIntire of Salem. In 1850 Richard S. Rogers acquired the complex. The property was sold to the Xavier Brothers in 1922. Prior to the sale, the Rogers family sold some of the interior rooms, renowned for their architectural features, to the Boston Museum of Fine Arts.

In the name of progress, bulldozers and a wrecking crane demolish the palatial Oak Hill estate, in April of 1956 for the future home of the North Shore Shopping Center.

Three
Street Scenes

In 1913 Peabody Square was a center of activity, with many shops. Prominent landmarks included the Soldiers Monument and the South Congregational Church.

In this stereoscopic view from the 1880s, a flagman has stopped traffic on Central Street so that the steam engine may cross.

The freight yard of the Peabody train station is shown here, c. 1890. The rear of the South Church can also be seen, and to its right is the train station.

By the time this photograph was taken in the 1910s, the depot had lost most of its decorative details. Other modes of transportation included the horse-drawn vehicles next to the trolley, and what is probably a Model T in front of the depot. Before the introduction of highways and truck freight, railroads were particularly important to the development of the leather industry. Four rail lines brought both passengers and freight to the town. Eventually these lines were absorbed by the Boston and Maine Railroad.

Boston and Maine Railroad service continued for many years. This photograph captures the last train departing the Peabody Depot for Boston on May 16, 1958. Note the dilapidated condition of the depot on the right.

This image, taken in the early 1880s, captures two enduring and prominent businesses in Peabody. On the left is the business owned by Benjamin F. Stevens, watchmaker, jeweler, and stationer, which was established in 1857 at 16 Main Street. The other, Albert H. Whidden's hardware business at 18 Main Street, dated from 1871. Notice the Woman's Christian Temperance Union above the hardware store. The WCTU was organized in 1875, and meetings were held every Friday at 3 pm.

A view of Main Street looking toward Salem, September 21, 1896. Notice the trolley approaching in the center of the street; electric railway service from Salem began in 1890.

This image of Foster Street dates to the 1890s. The second building on the right at #19 contained D.B. Lord's Plumbing business, which was a fixture on the street from the 1880s through the first decade of the twentieth century.

Main Street leads into the Square, c. 1907. The Allen Block served as offices for lawyers, insurance agents, and real estate agents, including Patrick J. Woods, who previous to dealing in this field had been a morocco dresser. Prominent stores included Raymonds (newsdealer and cigar shop), and Lundergan's (shoe dealer), and Gardner's (harness makers).

A bird's-eye view shows the residential area of Peabody, with its many fine homes and churches. Note the landmark water tower in the center of the photograph on Buxton's Hill.

This is another birds-eye view of Peabody, as seen from Buxton's Hill, showing the many tanneries in full operation as well as the dwellings of the workers in the foreground.

The trolley system in Massachusetts was extensive. A sign on the open car in the top photograph states that one could travel to Ipswich, Essex, and Gloucester by easy connections. Electric streetcar service from Salem began in 1890, and the Wakefield Street Railway was opened to Peabody in 1898. Streetcars running to Lynn were inaugurated in 1883.

This photograph was taken at the corner of Main and Foster Streets before 1899. The photograph can be dated by the J.W. Trask Co. Provisions at #5 Main Street, which was only in business from 1896 to 1899. The store specialized in meats, butter, tea, and coffee.

Amateur photographer George F. Low, a bookkeeper working in Boston, took this photograph looking west from the front stairs of the General William Sutton house in the 1890s. This image shows how the estate was being encroached upon by other buildings as time proceeded. The tall building on the right is the Wallis School, and in the foreground the Albert L. Kraus Company, the George Foan Company, and the W.P. Clark & Company, morocco and sheepskin manufacturers on Pierpont Street.

Three carriages of graduated sizes, from a one-seater to a three-seater are posed on Foster Street in this photograph from the 1890s. Patrick Buckley's Boots, Shoes, & Rubbers, located at #21 Foster Street was in operation here from 1890 until it moved to the Allen Block after 1907.

This is a view of the side yard at 56 Northend Street. This saddled pony with festive bows on its mane supports the infant Ida Espinola. Next to her is her mother Sarah, followed by older sisters, Mary and Alice. Ida married Stanley Swiderski of Peabody in 1936, and together they had four children, Janet, Kathrine, Stanley, and Alice. (Photograph c. 1915, courtesy of Elaine F. Cutler.)

Chestnut Street appears peaceful in this c. 1907 photograph. A portion of City Hall can be seen on the right, and on the left is the J.B. McManus Funeral Home. Previous to entering this line of business, McManus had been a butter peddler for many years.

Proctor's Crossing was considered a village in the 1890s. A prominent landmark was the Emerton Farm. The 33-acre farm included a silo, the house and barn on the left, and on the right a cider mill. In 1898 Charles S. Emerton sold the property, and later that year J.B. Eaton and Company leased the cider mill and reopened it for business. By the summer of 1899 the mill was being converted into a summer cottage.

This photographic print of Lowell Street dates from around 1890. On the right is 237 Lowell Street, the Jonathan King House. On the left is 240 Lowell Street, the home of Mr. & Mrs. Eden King, adopted daughter Alice, and son Warren. "Warren was in M.I.T. and when at home rode his horse furiously up and down Lowell Street." He later became superintendent of the Peabody Municipal Electric Light Plant. Mr. King was a determined opponent of spendthrift politicians and could be depended upon to oppose them vigorously in town meetings.

This Hussey-Holden House (before 1892), on the corner of Lynnfield and Summit Streets, shows the decidedly rural character still to be found in the city at that time. This photograph can be dated after 1892 by the electrical street lights, which were first lit on September 27, 1892. This house was torn down and replaced by a business block in the early 1960s. Next to this is Holden's Oil Company and Gas Station.

Wilson Square was a gathering place for young boys in 1903. Some of the boys seem to be playing marbles. Note the horse trough on the left, and the boy pumping the water.

The Benjamin Wilson house, shown at the extreme left in this c. 1903 photograph, was built before 1798. Notice the trolley tracks which ran along Andover and Central Streets.

This view of Lynnfield Street shows a much earlier time when horse-drawn wagons were the main source of business and private transportation. The tracks on Lynnfield Street show that the most popular form of public transportation was the trolley.

Here, Irving Goodell Small, an Army Staff Sergeant in Ordinance during World War II, poses in the back yard of the family home with his father, Elwin Lloyd Small, a clerk in the lighting department of General Electric. The house, located at 27 Columbia Boulevard, was purchased around 1920 and seems to have been photographed at lilac time. (Photograph courtesy Irving G. Small.)

In this photograph, Clayton Lloyd Small, a Motor Machinist First Class in the U.S. Navy during World War II, pats the family dog. His mother, Marjorie Perry Pitman Small, and her cat pose for her husband Elwin Small on the front steps of their home at 27 Columbia Boulevard in South Peabody. (Photograph courtesy Clayton L. Small.)

A 1954 photograph of downtown Peabody shows a thriving shopping district, bustling with activity. Note the many prominent stores, including W.T. Grant's, First National Stores, Raymond's Pharmacy, and A.H. Whidden & Sons.

Four
Recreation and Celebrations

Summer cottages nestled into a sylvan knoll near the placid waters of Bartholomew Pond in South Peabody. The pond was named after Richard Bartholomew, an early-seventeenth-century settler who owned the pond and surrounding rocky area. The rustic cottage on the left is the Harrison cottage c. 1890.

General William Sutton was born on July 26, 1800, in Peabody, and rose to prominence as a wool manufacturer. His military career of forty-seven years of service began at age seventeen, when he joined the Salem Cadets. He became a brigadier general in 1841. Archer H. Townley dedicated a military waltz to him. His estate, which was built in 1839, was located on a hill between Main and Aborn Streets. Marching up the driveway are the Salem Cadets led by a band of about twelve pieces. There seems to be five ranks in close order, with muskets carried in an upright position. On the lawn of the mansion's Main Street side are six conical tents, with a larger tent in the center.

The Essex Agricultural Fairs were held in Peabody from 1895 to 1909 in an area near Emerson Park. Buildings were constructed for the exhibition of various types of livestock, fruits, vegetables, and flowers. In 1910, the Essex Agricultural Society was bequeathed the Treadwell Farm in Topsfield, and the yearly fairs have been held there since. These photographs date to around 1903.

Bartholomew's Pond is about 8 acres in size and is surrounded by pine trees and a high rocky cliff covered with oaks. There is a legend that at various times the spirit of Menomee appears on the granite cliff. Menomee was a young and beautiful Indian maiden who lived with Minister Whiting and family in Lynn in 1654. Her Indian lover, so says tradition, was drowned while fishing from the great sliding rock on the shores of this pond, and she, crazed and heart-broken, left home and friends, and while wandering where she had spent so many happy hours with the one she loved, threw herself from the cliff and was drowned in the deep waters beneath. (Photographs courtesy Lynn Historical Society.)

Ship Rock, a geological granite wonder known as an erratic, is a 2,200-ton deposit off Summit Street left by the melting glaciers. It was a gift from Caleb Osborn and wife to the Essex County Natural History Society on November 3, 1847. The one-acre site is now owned by the Peabody Essex Museum. Some people say it got its name because it resembles a hull of a ship, while another theory is that a group of sailors deserted their ship in Salem and used this area as a hideaway. Others believe that pirates used it as a lookout to Salem Harbor and surrounding areas.

This is an 1886 woodblock engraving of Cliff Rock in South Peabody near the Lynn line. South Peabody is located on rugged rocky terrain dotted with many glacial erratics. This huge and formidable granite cliff is menacing to hikers and was nearly inaccessible during the nineteenth century. (Photograph courtesy of Sandra DeGrazia.)

Here, Kate Sawtell Walker (left) poses with a guest during tea in her elegant home at #1 Warren Street. The Walker home, built in 1870, contained all the modern conveniences, including the first telephone in Peabody.

The Women's Chorus posed for this *c.* 1918 photograph at the Peabody Institute Library, while surrounded by potted palms and under the watchful eye of George Peabody.

Soprano soloist Mary Davies Durland, and speaker, accompanist Bessie Raymond Buxton, performed "Songs and Stories of Bonny Scotland" at the Peabody Institute. Buxton, known for her lectures on horticulture, spoke throughout New England. She was the author of several books, and was founder and first president of the Peabody Garden Club. Bessie Buxton was a talented pianist and organist who appeared in many programs.

"Skippers Yarns with Sailor Chanties" was the title of a program arranged by Bessie R. Buxton. Mrs. Buxton researched sea charities by meeting with sea captains and sailors. She often presented programs combining stories and songs.

An early spring outing on the shores of Suntaug Lake, was captured in this April 19, 1897 photograph.

This view shows the calming shores of Suntaug Lake at the Peabody-Lynnfield line. Named Humphrey's Pond after John Humphrey, an early settler who was granted 1,500 acres in the early 1600s, the name was later changed back to its Indian name. The city of Peabody purchased the lake for use as a reservoir. Prior to that it was a popular site for boating, swimming, fishing, and ice harvesting.

Manuel and Sarah Cunha Espinola were married at St. John's the Baptist Church in Peabody on September 7, 1907. Both were born in the Azores Islands and immigrated to Peabody at a very young age. They lived for a time at 56 Northend Street, where their six children, Mary, Ida, Sarah, Jerome, Dorothy, and Alice were born. (Photograph courtesy of Mr. and Mrs. Roger Slate.)

A whimsical photograph was taken on February 1, 1897, at the home of Herbert H. Buxton at 9 Andover Street. Pictured here are, from left to right: Henry Hallberg, Helen Roberts, Bessie Buxton, Ernest Porter, and Sadai Porter.

This *c.* 1890 photograph, taken at the Pevear Estate on Main Street in front of the stables shows attractive young girls dressed as old ladies. From left to right are: (front row) Helen Jacobs and Freda Upton; (back row) Louise Teague, Rena Wilson, Rose Watkins, Betty Campbell, and Bertha Clark.

This Halloween Party in the attic of 9 Andover Street took place on October 31, 1897, and was hosted by Herbert H. Buxton.

An 1897 April Fool's Day party was held in the front parlor of the Nathan Bushby House, at 75 Central Street. The party was hosted by Miss Helen W. Roberts, the owner of the historic property.

Members of the Unity Club dressed for a costume party held at the Unitarian Church on Park Street, c. 1890.

For the Armistice Day celebration, November 11, 1918, workers left the factories to rejoice in the Square. All the factory whistles, fire alarms, and church bells were used to announce the armistice. Twenty-six Peabody men were killed in World War I.

Upton Building, at the corner of Foster and Lowell Streets was traditionally decked out in flags and bunting for civic events. Here the town welcomes home its soldiers and sailors from World War I on June 14, 1919. The festivities included boxing bouts, a large parade, band concerts, and a military ball.

This portrait of Jessie Cunha of Peabody was taken in 1919 during World War I in France. Private Cunha is preparing to savor the bouquet of a Burgundy during a break from the war. (Photograph courtesy of Borinous Schier.)

Little Mary Espinola, surrounded by her escorts, posed for the photographer before marching in the Holy Ghost Parade. The Holy Ghost Parade is held on Pentecost Sunday, the seventh Sunday after Easter. (Photograph courtesy of Elaine F. Cutler.)

Members of the Friscos Athletic Club are pictured in 1935 in front of a huge bonfire made from tannery barrels. The club was located at 20 Northend Street. Pictured are, from left to right: (front row) Fred Sweeney; Jack Sweeney; Bucky Amaral; Joe Silva; Ray Levasseur; Mike Butler; Frank Rosa; Dinny Wiggin; and Frank Butler; (back row) Bill Walsh; Jeff Horrigan; Alec Dragon; Bruno Dubowicz, Pete Dratus; Carnival Guy; Jim Dratus; Bill Sylvester; Al Perakis; Tom O'Rouke; and Frank Narbis.

This c. 1956 photograph shows the Holy Ghost Parade. The Portuguese community was a strong presence in the city, and one of their main celebrations has been this parade. Children dressed in white march along with adults, who carry the three crowns, soon to be bestowed on the young girls. A marching band can be seen in the background. (Photograph courtesy Anna Ortins.)

Everyone loves a parade. Here, bystanders line up along Lowell Street in the 1950s as a parade marches by. Note Lalime's Garage at 25 Lowell Street in the background.

Pictured here is a Patuleia Family birthday party, c. 1956. Rufino Patuleia of Shillaber Street usually celebrated with one party for three of his children since they were all born around the same date. Here the family take a moment from their celebrations to pose for a photograph. (Photograph courtesy Anna Ortins.)

50TH ANNIVERSARY
PORTUGUESE BENEFIT SOCIETY
OUR LADY OF HELP
- PEABODY, MASSACHUSETTS -
- AUGUST 15, 1954

A 50th anniversary banquet was held in Peabody, August 15, 1954, to celebrate the Portuguese Benefit Society, Our Lady of Help. Begun in the first decade of the twentieth century, the

Society was formed to help the many immigrants arriving from the Azores and Portugal. (Photograph courtesy Sally Nicosia.)

Comedian Jerry Lewis was at the peak of his popularity when he entertained for a packed house at the opening of the newly completed Northshore Shopping Center Cinemas in 1963.

A Boston Red Sox baseball team tribute was held in Peabody in 1967. Seated in the back seat of the Ford convertible are Dick and Norma Williams and Mayor Edward Meaney. The United States Marine Corps certainly had the crowd under control.

Imposing and vividly painted wooden sentries stood guard during the holiday season at
Northshore Shopping Center, c. 1965. Jordan Marsh and Filene's were the key anchor stores for
the center. The building contract was awarded to the John A. Volpe Construction Co. in 1957.
On September 12, 1958, the $10 million dollar complex was dedicated. More than 50,000
thousand people attended this auspicious event.

Five
Business as Usual

Dole and Osgood Company was located on Washington Street. Presumably, Dole and Osgood made the carriages for the annual promotion for "Moxie." The company, established in 1834, was founded by William T. Dole, who took W.E. Osgood as partner. The partners built up an extensive trade in wagons and carriages. The company did much business with Australia and the Sandwich Islands, and sold a six-seated carriage to the Queen of the Sandwich Islands.

The large brick building on the right was the mansion of Richard Crowinshield. The house, built in 1815, had a secret passageway via an underground tunnel that connected his fashionable home to his woolen mill. Later the Sanger Glue Factory took over the site. In the 1890s, Arthur C. Lawrence purchased the complex for his leather company.

This is an interior view, *c.* Oct. 1914, of the Samuel E. Knapp Morocco Factory at 12 Hanson Street. Still working at his trade at age seventy-five is James T. Turner of 46 Aborn Street.

Spring Pond is part of Peabody's reservoir system but in the early part of this century its shore was lined with ice houses. Cutting ice was a large industry in New England until the 1930s. Several Lynn companies, including Z.J. Chase and Sons and the M.S. Coolidge Ice Company, used area ponds for ice harvesting. (Photograph courtesy Lynn Historical Society.)

The abundance of good clay along the banks of the Waters River was ideal for the manufacturing of utilitarian pottery in Peabody and Danvers. Shown in the warehouse interior are examples of various finished products.

George H. Jacobs, Clothier, Hatter, and Furnisher, 25–27 Main Street, was established in 1884. This turn of the century image shows the exterior of the shop. Described in an 1893 publication as "a wide thriving trade built up based on first class goods and unvarying liberal dealings. He has a handsomely fitted up store . . . and employs three experienced and courteous assistants. Those who desire the most tasty, neat and stylish garments in every way equal in fit, material and wearing power to those obtained at any tailor's will be thoroughly gratified upon examining the goods and the fair modem prices at this store."

The United States Tanned Pigskin Company was located on Main Street. The company was owned by Frank Winchester, who enlarged the building from two stories to nine stories. One of the company's specialties was the manufacturing of tanned pigskin hides for covering footballs, using a closely guarded secret process. The structure was demolished for safety reasons because of architectural problems with the building leaning to one side.

This *c.* 1915 view of the Boston and Maine Railroad freight office on Railroad Avenue shows employees busily working in their modern office, complete with a candlestick-style telephone and overhead incandescent lighting.

The Danvers Bleachery and Dye Works, at 119 Rear Foster Street, was owned by the Naumkeag Steam Cotton Company of Salem. At the bleachery, the material from the Salem mill was bleached, stitched together, starched, dyed, ironed, and folded.

National Calfskin employees at the Webster Street factory show their patriotic spirit as they prepare to march in support of Liberty Bonds, perhaps during World War I. Notice the tricomer hats, flags, and scepters.

The oldest store in town, located at what is now 138 Main Street, was established in 1735. The first shop keeper was John Southwick. Over the years the building was remodeled and enlarged and had a variety of occupants. The Batchelder family operated the general store for over seven decades. The stage coach and trolley used this store as a stop. In the 1920s, this venerable building was demolished to make way for a gas station.

Members of the United Leather Workers Local No. 1 posed for a photograph in September 1918. Peabody's main labor organization, Local No. 1, met every second Thursday at 7 Central Street. Notice that their badges are in the shape of a leather hide.

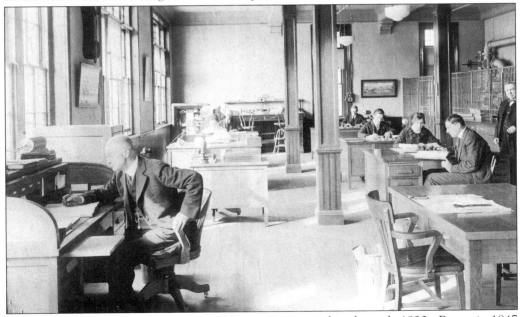

The Danvers Bleachery office is pictured here as it appeared in the early 1920s. Begun in 1847 and closed over a hundred years later in 1953, this plant had bleached over 100 tons of goods by 1855, according to historian John A. Wells. From its beginnings as a single story building, the business grew into a large complex, at one time employing over 1,000 people.

This *c.* 1920s photograph shows the Griess-Pfleger Tanning Company office at 7 Howley Street. Seventy-one firms in Peabody operated in the leather trade, including 4 leather embossers, 2 leather findings, 2 leather finishers, 42 leather manufacturers, 5 leather remnants, 4 leather tanners, and 4 companies classified in the city directory as leather. There were also 4 tanners listed, 1 each of tanning extracts and tanner oils and greasers, and 3 tanner's supplies.

Workers are finishing patent leather at the Waters River plant of A.C. Lawrence Leather Company on Pulaski Street in this *c.* 1920s photograph. Peabody's history is closely tied to the history of tanning in America, and Arthur C. Lawrence is credited with making Peabody the leather capital of the world. The company was formed in 1894 for the manufacture of sheep leather, and later expanded into calf leather and several other types. The company included a main plant on Crowinshield Street, facilities on Endicott and Pulaski Street. Over 3,000 people were employed at the peak of manufacturing.

This March 1931 photograph shows Crystal Lake Farm, on Goodale Street, in West Peabody. The proprietors were John L. and Rena H. Carten and Son. The Victorian home has an impressive veranda. Impeccably maintained, the farm had an extensive network of farm buildings.

Peabody was home to several dairy farms in the early 1900s. This is an interior view of the large dairy barn of the Crystal Lake Farm, c. 1931.

This photograph dated April 7, 1908, shows the John E. Herrick Dairy Farm, on Winona Street, including a partial view of the house and large barn with three cupolas, as well as outbuildings. Tragedy struck in 1902, when a disgruntled employee robbed the Herrick home and set fire to the barn, killing more than two dozen cows. In 1948, the old Foster-Herrick homestead, built *c.* 1775, was destroyed by a devastating fire. The old farm and the land were developed into housing, and today the area is known as the Herrick Estates.

Seated at a roadside stand at Five Corners, Lake, Pine, and Winona Streets, are the proprietors, Stuart and Clara A. Bell, *c.* 1927.

The Upton Block, corner of Foster and Lowell Streets, is pictured here *c.* 1920. Foster Hotel can be seen on the left. The block contained the well-known Manning's Lunch, as well as the offices for Kirstein's Leather Company, whose factory was on Walnut Street.

Hotel Foster on Foster Street, the last of the old time hotels, had been in business from the early 1900s. In the 1930s, the hotel was converted into a post office and apartments. In the 1960s, the building was torn down for a municipal parking lot.

The gas station pictured here, Wilson Square Auto Supply, at 1 Andover Street, was built on the original site of the Benjamin Wilson house. From left to right are: Lester R. Spicer, John Mullarkey; and Ralph Blair. Spicer, Mullarkey and another partner, Lawrence Madison purchased the business in 1938.

Frederick E. Mercer, the proprietor of Mercer's Filling Station and Garage, at 73 Lynn Street, c. 1945, had a full-service gas station selling Mobil gasoline and also offered complete automotive repairs. The family lived further down at 186 Lynn Street.

Carnalino Consoli was president of Wakefield Palm Garden, Inc., at 221 Andover Street. The popular restaurant offered the finest foods and liquors, as well as dancing to McFarland's Orchestra and two floor shows nightly.

The Famous Wakefield

Palm Garden

NOW IN PEABODY

On Route 114, Andover and Sylvan Streets

The same friendly atmosphere and congenial hosts and waitresses that made our Wakefield Palm Garden famous

Finest Foods and the Best Liquors
Dancing to McFarland's Orchestra
Two floor Shows Nightly

For Reservations Call Peabody 1054

Pictured at Al's Diner, 94 Foster Street, c. 1940, are, from left to right: Alex O. Brunet, (owner), Peter Desjardins, and Oscar Belle, Sr. Al's Diner, a Worchester style diner, was originally on Main Street. (Photograph courtesy Gary Thomas.)

Working together at toggling leather are, from left to right: Frank Wisegood, Albert Fermon, Harold McDonald, and Leo Pernitchi. Toggle hooks are a device used for gripping the edge of a hide or skin when it is suspended from a rack for drying or stretching. Before toggle-drying developed in the early twentieth century, the skins were dried after being nailed out onto boards. The nails were made of brass or galvanized iron, and were thickened with short wooded sleeves under their heads to prevent tearing the skin. (Photograph courtesy North Shore Jewish Historical Society.)

Central Pool and Billiard Parlor, 7 Central Street, corner of 6 Walnut Street, was located on the third floor and was owned by Joshua Yonis of 133 Main Street. The spacious hall had hardwood floors, stark walls, a dozen billiard tables, a jukebox, and glaring fluorescent lights.

The Towne-Lyne House Restaurant, Route 1, Peabody, at the Lynnfield line, is situated high above the shores of Suntaug Lake. On August 31, 1954, Hurricane Carol devastated the New England states. The force of the hurricane's power is evident in this photograph, as the high velocity winds easily uprooted this mature deciduous tree. (Photograph courtesy Warren Falls.)

The Bel Aire Diner, at 131 Newbury Street, was built in 1952 for Peter and William Kallas. The diner was constructed in New Jersey and moved to the site. This well-known Route One landmark is larger than most diners, having a seating capacity of 106. According to the present owner, Harry Kallas, the Bel Aire Diner is one of only 450 models of its type remaining in the continental United States. (Postcard courtesy of Gary Thomas.)

Alpers Store, Incorporated, at 10 Foster Street, a popular men's clothing store for many years, was owned by Hyman Alpers of Salem. The store closed in 1989. (Picture *c.* 1955; courtesy of North Shore Jewish Historical Society.)

Alice Vagge Gowns, 7 Andover Street at Wilson Square, a remodeled Victorian building housing a popular and stylish woman's store, specialized in formal gowns for all occasions. Prom girls, potential brides and their attendants were enthralled by the dazzling array of ever changing window decorations. (Picture *c.* 1956; courtesy of Ben & Sally Mathias.)

Pictured here are charming and lovely representatives of Holiday Bowling Lanes and North Shore Cinema, at Northshore Shopping Center. This publicity pose made it hard to resist patronization of these establishments.

At Northshore Shopping Center, decorated for the holiday season, festive lights and displays enticed shoppers to the key anchor stores of Filene's and Jordan Marsh.

An aerial view depicts the A. C. Lawrence Leather Company complex during its conversion into housing for the elderly. Arthur C. Lawrence founded the company in 1894. Within a few years the company became the largest producer of sheep leather in the city. (Photograph taken August 6, 1974; courtesy of the *Lynn Daily Evening Item*.)

South Essex Sewerage District employee Alphonso Grigonis (1920–1994) drives past the sewer treatment facility (called a grease and grit chamber) located at the corner of Howley and Grove Streets. The building was destroyed by fire and the area covered over. The SESD headquarters were located on Fort Avenue in Salem.

Six

Public Safety

This is a group photograph of uniformed members of Steamer 2, Peabody. An interesting part of the uniform is the white leather belt emblazoned with the city's name.

The Peabody Police Department is pictured here as they appeared in November 1896. A police force consisting of one day man and six night men was established in 1877. The police station, originally situated in the fire house on Foster Street, moved to the Town Hall in 1883, where this photograph was taken.

Peabody Police marched in a parade for the Farmers Festival on September 22, 1897. The festival included a cattle show and fair as well as the parade, firemen's muster, and bicycle races.

Chief of Police William Fred Wiggin was promoted to chief from patrolman in 1896 and served as chief from 1896 to 1899, when he was transferred to the night force.

This rare action photograph of Hose Company #1 rushing to a fire was taken on Lowell Street, sometime between 1905 and 1909. The company was stationed at 37 Lowell Street.

The Lynn Street Fire Station, in South Peabody, was built in 1875. Pictured here is Engine 5, a 1916 LaFrance pumper. Standing from left to right are: John McDonald; France Kellett; Al Larrabee, and George Hodgdon. The firehouse was destroyed by fire on April 14, 1961.

Firefighters stand in front of the Hose 2 Fire Station on Washington Street, *c.* 1915.

A group of firefighters in dress uniform posed in front of the Central Fire Station. Standing, from left to right are as follows: Charles Hurd, Charles Thomas, Charles Caden, William Murphy, Henry W. Lawrence, Captain John J. Keefe, Chief Jesse L. Barrett, Arthur R. Emerson, Edward Ingalls, and Frank Berry. Standing on the hook and ladder truck are: Joseph L. Mulcahy, Cornelius J. Duggan, and William C. Mahoney. Seated behind the wheel is Daniel J. Hannan, and beside him is George Morgan. The Seagrave hook and ladder truck was the first motorized piece of fire equipment in Peabody. It was purchased by the town in 1908.

The Central Fire Station, on Lowell Street, was built in 1873. Pictured at the wheel in this 1914 photograph is the town electrician and superintendent of the Fire Alarm Department, Vincent O'Keefe. Seated next to him is Chief Engineer Jesse F. Barrett. In the rear seat, from left to right are: Assistant Engineers Arthur P. Bodge, Thomas Hutchinson, John Costello, and Thomas Carbrey.

This photograph of firefighters was taken in 1916 in front of Hose 3 on Endicott Street. From left to right are: Fred W. Bodge; guest T.B. Bagley, Frank Toye, George P. Bodge (rear) H.B. Buxton, Freeman P. Bodge (driver), Benjamin H. Bodge, Louis Saxton, Frank L. Dunham, Samuel Watts, Arthur Bodge, and Jesse Barrett. In July of 1988 the City Council gave the decommissioned fire station to the Peabody Historical Society. A group of dedicated volunteers dismantled, moved, and rebuilt the historic structure at Brooksby Farm.. The bell tower was hoisted in place on July 8, 1994. The exterior work has been completed and most of the interior work nearly completed.

The A.B. Clark fire of April 28, 1909, started in the big eight-story wooden building of the sheep leather plant. In a few minutes it was a roaring mass of flames. A heavy rain prevented the fire from spreading to the National Calfskin Company.

The ruins of the American Glue Company off Washington Street are the result of a two-alarm fire that started in a storehouse of the glue company on May 8, 1906. The one-story wood-frame structure, built in 1885, was completely destroyed. There were about 2,000 barrels of glue in the building, most of which were lost. The winds carried the flames away from the main factory, causing it to be spared.

Hose Company #3, at 7 Endicott Street, was built 1876. The driver of the engine was Freeman Bodge. The company was made up of ten members. The photograph was taken c. 1910.

Pictured here are E. Lawrence Durkee and Ruby Irene Durkee, volunteer firefighters for West Peabody Pine Street Station.

The Central Fire Station, Hose Co. No. 1, was built in 1873 at 37 Lowell Street (later 41). This photograph, c. late 1950s, shows the state of the art equipment.

Peabody's State Guard Security Unit are standing at attention on the steps of City Hall, in this November 1943 photograph. The unit was commanded by Capt. F.H. Moore (front right.) Each unit was trained for the defense of a specific community.

This is a view looking toward Central Street during the 1954 flood. Flooding is no surprise to Peabody residents familiar with the area. Flooding has occurred in January 1978 and 1979, April 1987, and as recent as October 1996.

On Sunday, May 16, 1954, heavy rains caused the bursting of a dam owned by Eastman Gelatine Corporation, flooding downtown Peabody. Foster Street, depicted here, was completely under water. Some areas were inundated by 6 feet of water.

Peabody City Hall, located on high ground, was somewhat spared by the flood.

This photograph shows Peabody Square as seen during the 1954 flood. The brick building with the square tower and mansard roof is the Fire Station on Lowell Street.

A flood inundated the centerfield area off Lowell Street. The Peabody Fire Department is preparing to rescue an unfortunate woman surrounded by flood waters. In the seventeenth century this area was part of "Groton," a 300-acre farm that belonged to the distinguished colonist Emanuel Downing. Downing's son George (1624–1684) was in the first graduating class at Harvard College in 1642. He left the Massachusetts Bay Colony a few years later to pursue a successful military and political career in England. Sir George was knighted by King Charles II in 1660. Downing Street in London is named after him.

In 1967 the Northshore Shopping Center hosted a reception for the Peabody residents who were members of the Boston Red Sox Championship Team. The Boston Red Sox manager, Dick Williams, and his wife are joined by members of the Peabody Police force. From left to right are officers Fleming, O'Keefe, Brown, Leger, Maguire, Witwicki, Chief Costello, and Officer Donlon.

The Gnecco and Grilk Tanning Corporation was located at 27 Howley Street. In 1964 a disastrous fire destroyed this building and took the lives of four people.

Here, Peabody Police Riot Squad, including Police Chief Joseph Donlon, practice their riot control techniques .

Well-known Peabody Police K-9 member "Skimo," the first K-9 assigned to the Peabody Police Department. Here the German Shepherd looks out the window of the cruiser of his partner, Officer Frank O'Donnell, c. 1960s.

Seven

Churches,
Public Buildings,
and Cemeteries

This is an interior view of the Unitarian church at Park and Summer Streets. The focal point of this church is the pipe organ of grandiose proportions.

Peabody City Hall, at 24 Lowell Street, was dedicated November 22, 1883. This Second Empire Victorian structure was designed by Rufus Sargent of Newburyport. The contractor was Joseph Parson and Company of Salem. The police station and court rooms were located on the lower level. The brick and granite structure is now listed on the National Register of Historic Places.

Pictured here is the Managing Board of Peabody, 1904. From left to right are: (standing) Charles S. Goldthwaite, P.J. Martin, and George A. Reynolds; (seated) Elmer M. Poor, Andrew N. Jacobs, and Richard J. Cullen. The members posed for this photograph at a studio. Note the painted backdrop.

The J.B. Thomas Hospital, on King Street, was designed by the Boston architectural firm of Kendall, Taylor, and Steven, and opened in 1907. The structure was named after Josiah B. Thomas (1827–1898), a prominent businessman who bequeathed $50,000 to the town for the construction of a hospital.

The Old Town Hall and High School on Stevens Street was built in 1854. This was the first town hall, and was used until 1883. It was also used as a high school until 1904, when a larger school was built on Central Street. In 1923, the city granted Fidelity Post #1011 Veterans of Foreign Wars use of the building for their headquarters.

The First Unitarian Church, at the corner of Park and Summer Streets, was organized January 1, 1825. The church was converted into condominiums in 1986.

The Old Universalist Church, at Walker Place, was organized April 6, 1832. The site is now occupied by the George Peabody Cooperative Bank.

The Rev. W.S. Sperry, pastor of the South Congregational Church, Peabody Square, is seated in his tastefully decorated Victorian study in this photograph.

Peabody's train station, located off lower Central Street, was quite handsome. The building boasted iron cresting on the ridgepole and decorative scalloped trim. The spurting fountain and two flower urns in full bloom complete this photograph from the turn of the century.

The Peabody Pumping Station was located at the back of Cedar Grove Avenue. A circular fieldstone tower with a raised roof supported by columns offered a panoramic view of the surrounding area.

The Old South Burying Ground, on Main Street at the Peabody-Salem line, pictured here c. 1890, was known in the seventeenth and early eighteenth centuries as the Trask Burying Ground.

Miss Elizabeth Whitman (1751–1788), of Hartford, Connecticut, checked into the Bell Tavern in May of 1788 using the name of Mrs. Thomas Walke. On July 10 she gave birth to a stillborn child, and died ten days later. She was buried with her child at the Old South Burying Ground. In 1797 a novel was published entitled *Coquette or the History of Eliza Wharton*, by Mrs. Hannah Foster. The novel resembled the life of Elizabeth Whitman. Over the years people would go to her grave and chip away souvenirs. By 1899 this was all that remained of the red sandstone marker.

The granite gravestone of General Gideon Foster (1749–1845) at Harmony Grove Cemetery on the Salem-Peabody line was donated by George Peabody. Harmony Grove Cemetery was part of Peabody from 1710 to 1856. In 1856, parts of Peabody land were exchanged for land owned by Salem in what is now South Peabody.

The first Jewish settlers arrived from Russia in 1896, and by the turn of the century there were fifteen Jewish families in the area. Religious services were first conducted in a building at the corner of Main and Mill Streets. Later, they were held in the Red Men's Hall on Foster Street. Congregation Sons of Israel was organized in 1909. The synagogue on Elliott Place and Sanborn Street was dedicated in 1913. (Photograph courtesy North Shore Jewish Historical Society.)

Morris Rosen appearing in *Bar Kochba*. In 1918, when this portrait was taken, the Hebrew school was just six years old. The school was under the sponsorship of the Congregation Sons of Israel. (Photograph courtesy North Shore Jewish Historical Society.)

Pictured here is the Peabody Hebrew School play, March 31, 1914. Performed in Peabody City Hall, *Bar Kochba* featured, from left to right, Alice Komarin, Locke Teacher, Sadie Sogoloff, Lillian Bernstein, Morris Rosen, Rose Rubin, and Jenny Salata. (Photograph courtesy North Shore Jewish Historical Society.)

Maple Hill Cemetery was established in 1916 to serve the growing Jewish population. The iron gate to the cemetery was forged by Samuel Tanzer, the only Jewish blacksmith in Peabody. His initials "S.T." can be found engraved on the slide bolt. (Photograph courtesy North Shore Jewish Historical Society.)

Pictured at the Banquet of the Peabody Hebrew Ladies Aid, *c.* 1955, are, from left to right: (seated) Mrs. Ida Pickman, Florence Kaplan, Frances Marron, and Shirley Young: (standing) Priscilla Lippa, Janice Cherney, Fay Davis, Mary Madow, Sally Wolsky, and Ruth Scholnick. (Photograph courtesy North Shore Jewish Historical Society.)

The cornerstone of the first catholic church in Peabody, St. John the Baptist Roman Catholic Church, at 17 Chestnut Street, was laid in 1871. The Gothic-style brick and granite building with its soaring steeple was completed eight years later in 1879. When completed, St. John was the largest house of worship in Peabody, a distinction it retains today.

Here, St. John's Boy Scout Troop dressed in their official uniforms stand at attention behind the rectory on Church Street.

South Congregational Church, on Peabody Square, was dedicated on August 10, 1844. It was built on the site of the former church, which was destroyed in the great Peabody Square fire of 1843. This Greek Revival edifice with its Ionic columns was razed in 1961. The District Court of Peabody occupies the site today.

This is a c. 1960 group photograph of members of the Jordan Lodge, Free and Accepted Masons. The hall was located on the third floor of the Warren Merchant Bank, on Main Street. The Masons received their charter in 1803 and met at Dr. Shed's home at 156 Main Street from 1816 to 1834. Today the Masons have their own building, Jordan Lodge, at 71 Wallis Street.

Cardinal Cushing paid a visit to St. Joseph's school in the early 1960's. St. Joseph's Roman Catholic Polish Church was dedicated on December 23, 1932, and the school opened on December 8, 1958. The school fell victim to low enrollments and the teaching sister closing in 1975. The church served the religious needs of Polish Americans for generations but, to great sadness in the community, closed on July 1, 1997.

Eight
Schools and Sports

Students of the South School are pictured here in the 1880s. South School was the last of four schools the town built as part of an appropriation of $120,000 for school construction. This building in South Peabody replaced the old Rockville School on Lynnfield Street and the primary school on Lynn Street.

Old District #6 School, also known as the Felton School, on Sylvan Street, was built in 1841. The building served as a schoolhouse until the 1930s.

With an open book in her hand and fifty-four pupils under her supervision, young Grace Maude Cone posed during the early winter of 1891 with the first-grade class on the front steps of the Wallis School, built on Sewall Street in 1869. (Photograph courtesy John Hardy Wright.)

A group of schoolchildren pose in front of the Thomas Carroll School on Northend Street. The school, built in 1913, was named for Thomas Carroll (1839–1914.) Born in Ireland, he came to Peabody as a young boy and received his education in the Peabody school system. In adult life he was involved in the leather and morocco industries. He served on various town committees, commissions, and was a state representative. (Photograph c. 1915; courtesy of Borinous Schier.)

This photograph of classmates and teachers at the Bowditch School on Central Street was taken in 1891. The school was dedicated in 1858, and was named for the famous mathematician and navigator Nathaniel Bowditch. Later the building was used by the American Legion.

The convent, school, and rectory of St. John's parish was photographed in 1905. Erected in 1893, the school was remodeled and enlarged in 1905. A tragedy occurred at St. John's Parochial School on October 28, 1915, when a fire which started in a closet under the stairwell destroyed the school while it was in session and took the lives of twenty-one children. An account was given by eyewitness Gertrude Bresnahan: "The scene was terrifying. At the front door were huddled perhaps 15 little girls and boys pleading to be rescued, yet no one could penetrate the wall of fire that separated the doorway from the yard. I saw the bodies of tots in flames, one with both arms extended and its clothing burning; this child was on the bottom of the pile."

This exterior view of Peabody High School on Central Street was taken c. 1935. The school, designed by the architect Edwin B. Balcomb, was built in 1904 and enlarged in 1920.

The Peabody High School Class of 1913, consisting of twenty-eight boys and twenty-eight girls, received their diplomas on June 24. Diplomas were given in five courses: Classical, Latin Scientific, Technical, English, and Commercial.

A kindergarten class of January 1920 appears pleased to pose for a photograph. Located at 10 Holton Street, the Peabody Community House Association ran classes as part of its services.

Pictured here is the Peabody High School football team of 1911. For many years baseball reigned supreme, but by the 1910s football came into its own. In 1916 and 1917, teams coached by Leander McDonald came to prominence, with the 1916 team going undefeated in its regular schedule.

Shown here is the champion football team of 1921. From left to right are as follows: (front row) Frank Hennesy, John Connelly, John Donahue, captain Ralph Holden, Costas Anosolos, Arthur Gavigan, and John Sweeny; (back row) Peter Panogopoulos, Joseph F. Luz, William Crean, and Mansfield Monro. Coached by Marty Donovan, the team won eleven games. The citizens of Peabody raised $5,000 to send the team to play an interscholastic game at Charleston, SC. Peabody was defeated 12–6.

The Center School on Franklin Street was dedicated at the end of the school year on June 13, 1870. The brick school building cost $45,000. Here the proud champions of the baseball team of 1921 pose with their trophy. The school was destroyed by fire in 1952.

Cast members of *Full House*, the senior class play of April 30, 1926, posed for this photograph. The Peabody High School Orchestra supplied the music in the production which was coached and directed by Miss Mary D. Sullivan.

The Peabody High basketball team is shown here in 1923, the first year varsity basketball was recognized as a major sport. The yearbook states, "This sport had been somewhat neglected in the past due to lack of a gymnasium, but upon the completion of a new building, facilities were provided for the development of a team."

The Center Grammar School Drum Corps posed for this photograph on June 4, 1937. The school was the only elementary school with such a program. Located on Franklin Street, it was dedicated on June 13, 1870, and destroyed by fire in 1952. The new Center School was dedicated in 1955, in a new location on Martha Terrace.

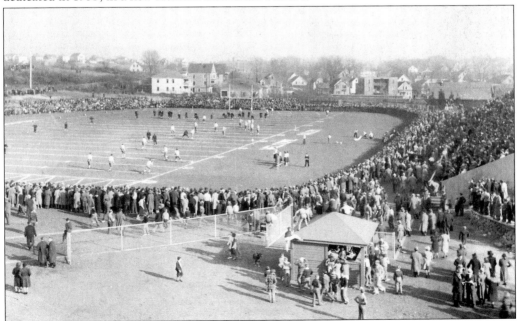

Crowds packed Leo Buckley Stadium on November 11, 1938. In this game, Peabody defeated Salem 20–6. The 1938 Peabody team won eight out of nine games played, with the ninth game being a tie with Gloucester.

Peabody High cheerleaders are pictured in this 1940 photograph. High school spirit always ran high, as this enthusiastic group of students shows.

The Peabody High School girls basketball team of 1939 poses for a team picture. Director of Girls Athletics Helen E. Riley turned out teams that were ranked with the best in the state.

This photograph shows girls athletics at Peabody High in 1939. A new club, the Apparatus Club was organized that year, with "more than 80 girls participating in various gymnastic exercises . . . During the course of the year the girls learned many dance routines among which was the 'Rufty Tufty.' "

Pictured here is a high school football game at Leo Buckley Stadium. The stadium was named in honor of quarterback Leo Buckley, considered one of the finest players ever at Peabody High. Buckley died of pneumonia in December 1922 while a student.

Richard Keon runs for a touchdown in 1944. Coach Bill Seeglitz produced a championship team that year. The team was undefeated, winning ten games and tying one on their way to winning the Class A title and Eastern Massachusetts Championship.

These members of the 1944 Peabody High School football championship team are Walter Roche, Richard Keon (standing), Tony Kravchuk, and Bob O'Connor (crouching).

Members of the Class of 1944 are pictured at their Junior Prom. The war raging in Europe affected everyone, occasionally even canceling school due to rationing.

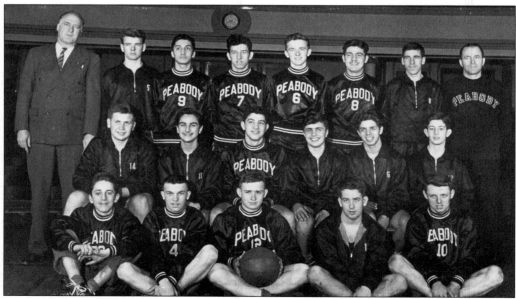

William Seeglitz, top left, coach of the basketball team of 1946, poses with Assistant Coach Eddy Donahue, top right. A young Nick Mavroules (No. 7, top row), who was later to be director of athletics, and eventually a congressman, along with Walter Sarowski (No. 6, to his right), were co-captains.

Peabody High School cheerleaders took a break from a football game at Manning Bowl, Lynn, in November 1946 to pose for this photograph. The Peabody team can be seen at the far left.

Among the members of the 1952 Peabody High School football team are Peter Torigian (No. 55, top left), who was elected mayor of the city of Peabody in 1979, and George Smyrnois (No. 37, lower row), the future director of athletics.

The 1949 Peabody High School hockey team posed for this photograph. According to the school yearbook the team "was off to a poor start when they dropped the first three games. However, they finished up strongly by winning four out of the next five for an even break of four victories and four defeats." From left to right are: (front row) Assistant Manager D. Donahue, P. Dook, R. Smith, R. Grayton, H. Alexuk, and Manager G. Donovan; (middle row) Coach Charles Carlin, Donald Price, R. Durkee, C. Mentus, and K. Mercer; (back row) O. Harriman, L. Broughton, A. Maguire, and J. Burke.

The high school band, "The Tanners," posed for a photograph in 1964. Sporting new uniforms, Drum Majorette Pat Maria and Baton Soloist Judy Stantial can be seen kneeling center foreground.

At one time, Peabody had two golf courses. The Salem Country Club on Lowell Street at Proctors Crossing was organized in 1897, and dissolved a few years later, about 1910. The other course, known as the Salem Golf Club, was located at the former Gardner Farm near Margin Street. The club was organized in 1895, and disbanded in 1925 when they moved to a new location at Forest Street under the name of the Salem Country Club.

The Warren Baseball Team of Peabody is pictured here in this c. 1900 photograph. Sports have long had a place in the history of the town, as these teams offered men from various professions a way of socializing. From left to right are: (front row) Pitcher Jack Phelan and Catcher Arthur Morgan; (middle row) Shortstop William McKean and Second Baseman Frank Littlefield; (back row) Third Baseman William Dooge, Center Fielder James Tyler, First Baseman Frank McKean, Substitute Pitcher and Right Fielder Genie Quinn, and Left Field Martin Quinlan.

In 1925, the Salem Country Club, newly organized and incorporated, purchased 750 acres of land from the heirs of the late Charles Sanders. The former Sanders Farms on Forest Street was transformed into a championship golf course. The course was designed by Donald Ross, and construction costs mounted to $175,000. This photograph, taken on May 27, 1925, shows the construction of the green on the 18th hole.

This is a *c.* 1955 photograph of junior golfers with their instructor at the Salem Country Club. Behind them is the clubhouse, built in 1926 at the cost of $155,000. The building was designed by architect and club member Gordon H. Robb.

Portuguese immigrants formed a soccer club, the Club Luis de Camoes, because of their deep love for the game. Pictured in this *c.* 1941 photograph are co-founders, Americo Lopes (second from left), Albert Lopes (fourth from left), and Rufino Patuleia (fifth from left.) (Photograph courtesy Anna Ortins.)

The ski slope at Page's Hill on Summit Street is pictured here. The 1,200-foot ski tow opened in the winter of 1950. The complex offered day and evening skiing. Today the area is part of the business center of Centennial Park.

John Bezemes, coach of the Peabody High baseball team of 1956–57, poses with his team. From left to right are: (front row) P. Pierce, N. Girgus, R. Enos, H. Velez, and L. Espindle; (middle row) C. St. Paul, E. McLaughlin, G. Moss, R. Wooldridge, D. Sullivan, A. Gibley, and L. Roumeliotis; (back row) D. Broughton, C. Speliotis, E. Bezzatti, and E. Callahan.

One of a number of Peabody Twilight Leagues, Frisco's Club was located at 20A Collins Street. In 1958, when this photograph was taken, the team consisted of, from left to right: (front row) Charles Wilkinson, James Riley, and John Egan; (middle row) Lou O'Keefe, Larry O'Keefe, Rich Codair, Frank Rossi, and Charles Speliotis; (back row) George Catarecs, Butch Galaris, Phil Anthony, ? Unid, Bill Callahan, and Cuppy Vlasuk.